STRATEGY TO SUCCESS

How To Live A Successful Life

by Steve Van Gard

CONTENTS

CHAPTER 1: Definition of success 1

CHAPTER 2: What Makes A Person Successful 9

CHAPTER 3: Success and Failure 16

CHAPTER 4: The Importance Of Mindset 23

CHAPTER 5: Your Strategy To Success 29

CHAPTER 6: Implement Your Strategy 34

CHAPTER 7: How To Overcome Obstacles 43

CHAPTER 8: Evaluate 51

CHAPTER 9: Success is Action 57

CHAPTER 10: Celebrate Your Success 62

CHAPTER 1: DEFINITION OF SUCCESS

"To laugh often and much;

to win the respect of intelligent people;

to appreciate beauty;

to find the best in others;

to leave the world a bit better, whether by a healthy child, a garden patch or a redeemed social condition.

To know even one life has breathed easier because you have lived.

This is to have succeeded"

– ***Success by Ralph Waldo Emerson***

When people are asked about their definition of success, most of them associate it with their careers, their professional lives, their businesses. For them, success means having money and achieving goals. At least that what we are taught in school. Even when it comes to students from primary school all the way to college, they are considered to be successful if they get good grades and if they win this competition of the grading system with their classmates.

An athlete is successful if he or she wins competitions and stays in the top performers, perhaps makes it to the Olympics, then that is real success.

A musician is successful if they sign a deal with a producer and become famous, sell millions of albums, get awards, shoot videos and get millions of Youtube views.

A lawyer is successful if he or she gets to win all the cases and makes partner in a firm.

A business owner is successful if they make six, seven or more figures in their business.

Success is more often than not also associated with fame. If someone else has heard of you, then you are definitely successful, you must be doing something right. And you must have the right amount of money in the bank account too.

Success is much more than that. Success does not come from a competition or comparison with someone else. You do not have to see someone fail in order for you to succeed. Success is personal.

Just like Emerson's poem from the opening of this chapter, success is about the footprint you leave behind, the way you touch people's lives and the impact and contribution you bring to this world. Living a successful life is about the happiness and joy, the laughter, the people you surround yourself with, appreciating and respecting the beauty of this life.

Success is all these things and includes the achievement of goals. After all, the dictionary definition of success is "the accomplishment of an aim or purpose". At the end of the day, it all comes down to what your purpose is. If you are chasing money and financial wealth, then you will define your success by the money in your account. If you have a purpose to impact people's lives, then you will define success by the number of people you encounter and form meaningful connections with.

Success is personal and you get to define it. If you come to think about it, there is no point to being rich if you are not enjoying yourself. Secondly, you are more likely to get rich if you are following your passions, making a contribution and being happy in the process. The feeling of lack and need will indeed move people to action. However, the action should be aimed at the objective of becoming happier and money will come.

"Try not to become a man of success. Rather become a man of value." -- Albert Einstein

Again, value is not reflected in the sum of money you make but it is about your personal values that guide you in life and that define you as a human being, who you truly are. When you are a person who sticks to their own values no matter what, then you will be able to see this as success, because integrity with your own set of values is essential.

"Stop chasing the money and start chasing the passion."-- Tony Hsieh

When you put passion into what you are doing, then it will not feel like you are working. When you are doing what you are truly passionate about, you will have the inner satisfaction that is a lot bigger than any sum of money.

"You know you are on the road to success if you would do your job, and not be paid for it." -- Oprah Winfrey

So if all these wise people are talking about success from a perspective of success beyond money and fame, then what is success? This is about you defining your own idea of success. Because success is about accomplishing your aims and objectives. But the only way of being successful in your pursue is to have this aim really clear for yourself.

We have already decided it is not about competing with anyone, it is not about seeing someone fail in order for you to win, it is not about comparing yourself with others. This means that success is about you. And you are the only one who can define it. Stop chasing someone else's definition of success. You are on your own journey. So make it your own.

Now try this exercise of introspection. What does success mean for you? What would make you really happy? What would make you celebrate your success? What is your vision? What is your purpose?

What is your mission? What makes you vibrate with joy? What is your passion? What triggers the real fire in your soul?

This is about you having a very clear picture of your own success. If you don't define success, someone else will define it for you. And you will not have the same feeling when you reach the goals that someone else is setting for you.

Think about for instance a sales person who needs to hit their target that month. The target is set by their manager. If they took a step back and looked at having a choice, would they really work towards meeting those targets? Or is there something else that would make them happy and feel like they have achieved something important? Sometimes, hitting some targets for someone else facilitates our road to our own success, but you have to keep it very clear in your mind what is your purpose and your definition of success. Do not get lost along the way. Do not get blinded by the instant gratification of hitting some targets when in the long run you are in fact killing your soul's targets.

Success could mean feeling that tingle of excitement about what you do, sticking with your values and what truly matters for you during hard times, living a life you can feel proud of in retrospect.

Success can only be defined from a personal point of view. You are responsible for your own happiness. You are responsible for your own life. You are responsible for defining your targets and your success. The below tips and quotes from successful people will guide you through this process.

"Ask yourself this question every morning: Will who you are now lead you to who you want to be in the future?

Avoidance is the best short-term strategy to escape conflict and the best long-term strategy to ensure suffering.

No matter how small you start, start something that matters.

Mediocrity begins the precise moment you swap love for challenge with love of comfort.

A meaningful life is just the sum of meaningful

moments. Live in every moment."

— ***How Incredibly Successful People Think* by Brendon Burchard**

"Make work a purpose, not just a place.

The pursuit of meaning—not happiness—is what makes life worthwhile.

The opportunity to do something you love will always be there, as long as you start today.

Spending on people and experiences yields the greatest return.

Focus on less to do more.

Trying to do a little bit of everything leads to doing nothing of substance."

— ***Are You Fully Charged: The 3 Keys to Energizing Your Work and Life* by Tom Rath**

CHAPTER 2: What Makes A Person Successful

If we look at the definitions considered in the previous chapter about success, then we already know the answer to "What makes a person successful" is not going to be an easy one.

Given that success is personal and individually defined, you can be successful by the way you see it. If your goal is to make one million dollars, then you might feel like a failure until you actually make that money. You might even miss all the fun along the way because you are too focused on the objective. And only when you hit the exact number of zeroes will you actually feel successful.

This is the type of life that you might not really be attracted to if your idea of success is more rooted into every day. Success is in the journey itself, not in the destination. Success is about winning everyday. Small wins and big wins. What is one thing you really enjoyed today. That makes your day successful.

With a continuously dynamic existence, we tend to be so focused on the outcomes, that we miss the chance to stay in the present moment and see the success in each and every step we take. Even when we experience a setback, we can still look at it as a successful lesson that will help us move forward in the long run.

Being successful can be about living a life that brings you happiness, being surrounded by the people who make you smile, giving and receiving love, having healthy relationships, working with passion, making an impact and leaving a legacy. Being successful today can simply be that moment when you laughed so hard that you could not stop for minutes in a row. Or you can think that joke interrupted you from sealing that deal and you missed your success because you took the time to laugh. This is why success depends on how you see it.

A successful person does not look different from you and me. They are regular people and they do the same things we do every day. They are though more grateful about what life brings into their daily existence.

They see success at every step and they live their life more fulfilling. They set achievable goals, but they also push themselves outside their comfort zones. They take action and yet they enjoy the ride. They learn the lessons and they never give up. They do not rely on material things to find their happiness and they do not set success on the back of their bank account.

"Successful people do what unsuccessful people are not willing to do. Don't wish it were easier; wish you were better." -- Jim Rohn

In order to be successful you must be willing to do the extra work, put in the extra effort, push yourself beyond the limits in order to become extraordinary. An ordinary person can become successful only by becoming better and better, only by becoming extra. The difference is that unsuccessful people have that resistance to failure that keeps them in a safety net and this way they give up too early because they are afraid of falling. But successful people will push through and always find solutions, always see opportunities, always get better and better.

Think about a person who has had an accident and might be in a wheelchair. They have a choice. They can either fall into depression and complain about what life has thrown their way or they can push through and become better at a skill that makes them extraordinary. They can either keep exercising to one day overcome their condition or they can find a way to inspire others in a similar situation. For them success can be being able to move their toes today. And that makes them successful and that is all they need. Or if they set a higher goal, it can be about that goal of taking part in a paralympics competition or being on television. No matter how big or small, their steps will make them feel successful depending on how they look at the situation.

Let's take another example. For instance, from the outside, a highly judgemental individual might think that a woman whose job is to be a housewife has missed her chance to be successful. She does not have a career and her husband is the one providing in the house, but this only reflects the faulty judgement of the outsider. The housewife is highly successful when it comes to managing the house, running the errands, raising the kids and perhaps even running her own business on the side. There are so many business mums nowadays. And they are successful. And their families are successful because they create all that space and environment every day. All members of the family are laughing, happy, nourished and loved and they themselves consider to be successful. And this is the most important part. How we end up defining ourselves is how successful we are.

"A successful man is one who can lay a firm foundation with the bricks that others throw at him." -- David Brinkley

To be honest, there will always be haters. They can show up when you are just starting your path and they might try to keep you away from risking. It might be out of love and trying to protect you, but they do not understand that by doing that they are actually cutting your wings. You know what you are capable of, so your path to success means not paying attention to them.

There will be others along the way who will make

you feel bad about the choices that you make, who will throw words of judgement and will try to put you down. Once again, you will be successful by feeling even more motivated to continue regardless of their judgements and misconceptions. The criticism will make you feel even more empowered and determined to follow your path to success. As Zig Ziglar puts it, "Don't be distracted by criticism. Remember--the only taste of success some people get is to take a bite out of you."

Getting yourself up and dusting yourself off, that is what the meaning of success is when it comes to creating your road.

When we were in school, teachers calculate our level of success with grades. And only if you get to be top of the class, you get to be called successful. Otherwise, you are just average. And we all seem to be living an average life if we do not strive for more. But the fact is, one student can be successful in his own field of interest, such as geography. Another one can be successful in chemistry. What happens is that sometimes success is judged based on a generic scale without looking closer at the specifics.

Just like in the housewife example, that person is successful in their own area of interest. She may not be successful in building cars, but she is successful in running the house and perhaps her own business.

Once again, success is individual. Success is personal and is based on what someone feels like they need to accomplish each and every day to feel they are closer to their big vision, to their dreams, to their goals. Success is achieving those goals, but also taking all the necessary steps along the way.

Being successful is about winning the day, surviving life and getting closer and closer to our dreams. What does being successful mean to you?

CHAPTER 3: SUCCESS AND FAILURE

There would be no success without failure, because success does not happen overnight. There is so much work and so many steps that need to be taken in order to become successful in any area of our lives.

For instance, you might be looking for the perfect romantic relationship. In young ages, we have an idea of the person we want to spend the rest of our lives with. Then we grow up, experience different types of relationships with partners who are at different stages of their lives and we fail and we get heartbroken. Until it clicks. Until we find true love. And then we can call ourselves successful on a romantic level.

It goes the same in all areas of our lives. We evolve and grow and learn throughout time and most of the times we will come to face failure more often than success. But that is how we shape our future selves.

If you were to win the lottery, you would be happy and you would spend the money. But would you call yourself successful? Maybe lucky, definitely worthy, but not successful. Because you did not really put effort, you did not risk and although you might have tried previous times, you still do not feel like a failure. I mean, let's face it, do you feel like a failure when you realise you did not win the lottery this week either? Not really, because there is no risk, and you know that there is only one chance, more that has to do with fate and destiny than with your success.

But when it comes to the way we live our life and the work we put into our professional life or relationships, then we know there are things we can do there to improve, to take action, to influence whether there will be some win or loss along the way. It is not just fate anymore, it is up to you as well.

In these situations, failing will definitely happen. No one can call themselves a continuous winner. The difference is in the way you respond to failure. If you let yourself be brought down by failure, then you will give up any other new chances to get back up and potentially win. If you instead go back in the game, you already are prepared to face failure, your skin gets thicker with every fall and you know these failures will only bring you closer to success. Because there is no success without failure.

Also, it is all in the perspective you give the failure. You might look at it as an obstacle, a setback, you might get frustrated, annoyed, upset, angry, or you might actually see it as a lesson. You learn what does not work and next time you know better. You learn what to do and what not to do.

"The real test is not whether you avoid this failure, because you won't. It's whether you let it harden or shame you into inaction, or whether you learn from it; whether you choose to persevere." -- Barack Obama

Whenever you set yourself up on a journey, you have to be prepared for whatever comes your way. It is very unlikely that you will succeed from the first attempt and even if you do, there will still be obstacles along the way. Also, no matter how much preparation you do, it is unlikely you will be able to cover with your imagination any possible scenario where things can go wrong. Something completely new might happen and you will have to face that failure and keep on going.

Sometimes, we enjoy something better if it comes with hard work. We appreciate it more and we are more aware that it is a precious achievement because we have put so much effort into it.

Think about the movies where the man tries to seduce the woman, he fails, he tries again but instead of impressing her, they end up fighting, he screws up, the relationship fails, then apologises, the relationship is now on track. And they lived happily even after. That is a successful ending, showing how hard it is to obtain something but also how beautiful it is to then enjoy the sweet taste of victory.

When it comes to our goals in life, we are so attached to them that we put all our hopes into the hands of fate and luck. And we do our best and most of the times we fail. But that is only to get ourselves prepared for a bigger purpose. This is to get ourselves back on track and constantly making sure we are still pursuing the right goal for us and that it still makes us happy to think about our success.

Even if we may not see it, success sometimes come disguised into a failure. We might be so focused on the goal to be achieved only in our own way that when there is an outcome that is slightly different to our expectation, we see it as a failure. Instead, it might be something much better than what you were imagining, but you were so stuck on that result that you just cannot look at anything else.

In the big picture of success as opposed to failure, we need to keep in mind that we always have options. We always have a choice of whether we move forward to back down. We always have a choice to look ahead or look back. We have a choice to see the outcome in front of us as a success or a failure, as a mistake or a lesson.

The important is to be aware all the time. The journey to success will be always impregnated with risks, decisions to make, ideas to put into action, setbacks, unexpected obstacles and even sabotage from other people or yourself. When we see the danger ahead and we are not prepared to face the failure, we might end up self sabotaging our own careers or relationships or goals just to avoid the disappointment. That is a mechanism of coping with failure that means avoiding failure and preventing it to happen by staying away from the risks. It means playing it safe. It means fear.

Fear is not going to bring you closer to success. Fear might keep you away from failure because you want to protect yourself, your business, the people around you, but fear will also keep you away from success. Because you will not be taking an opportunities from fear of the unknown. And there is no way to succeed without trying, without taking those opportunities and facing the uncertainty. And also failing. As a Japanese proverb says, "Fall seven times and stand up eight."

Probably one of the most encouraging pieces of advice to be given when it comes to the strategy of success and the roadmap to achievement is about making as many mistakes as possible. It makes the journey more interesting and it also prepares you for anything that may come along the way. Failure brings you closer to success.

"Would you like me to give you a formula for success? It's quite simple, really: Double your rate of failure. You are thinking of failure as the enemy of success. But it isn't at all. You can be discouraged by failure or you can learn from it, so go ahead and make mistakes. Make all you can. Because remember that's where you will find success." -- Thomas J. Watson

Go ahead, make mistakes and dive into the opportunities. Knock on the doors, deal with rejection, fail and get up again and again and again. This will only teach you something new every single day and it will bring you closer to success in any form it may come. Just make sure you do not miss it and confuse it with failure.

When it will appear after a series of failures, success will just taste so much better, and you will be able to enjoy it from a place of growth and development, ready to face any new challenges that may arise.

CHAPTER 4: THE IMPORTANCE OF MINDSET

When we decide to set ourselves up for success, there are a few steps we need to be taking. So once you have identified your goal that you want to achieve and the areas of your life where you want to be successful, you are now preparing for the journey. And before you hit the road, you need to see what you are packing to bring with you.

No matter if you are wishing for success in relationships, in your business or in becoming famous for one of your hobbies, you will need the most crucial tool in your box. You will need to make sure you are embarking on the journey to success with the right mindset.

Thoughts create our reality and we are in full control of what comes out of our brains. If we think we are not good enough to deserve to be successful, then our brain will continuously find solutions to this by showing you all the way in which you are failing. Instead, if you know that you are worthy of achieving anything you put your mind to, then no matter how many problems will appear in your way, your brain will find solutions to solve those problems and bring you closer to success. Because your reality is that you are achieving your success every day, step by step.

Our thoughts can either make us or break us. That is why our mindset plays such a big role in accomplishing or not our goals. When we think it is difficult, we will easily find ways to self sabotage our road to success. We will find some rocks to throw to the windows and break them, we will find something sharp to poke our tyres, anything that we can do in order to delay ourselves from moving forward because we do not deserve to reach that destination of success. We will manufacture distractions and our mind will continue to find it more entertaining to bring to front all the setbacks instead of bringing the wins into conversation.

The power of our thoughts is amazing. We still like to deceive ourselves that we do not have control over our thoughts. Because our thoughts seem scary. But what seems even scarier is that we have access to them and we can focus on shifting them into more pleasant, more welcoming, more motivational and inspirational thoughts that will support us in our journey to success instead of sabotaging it.

Just as we were discussing in the previous chapter, the mindset is the one that will decide the way we behave in front of failure. The perspective we get to have comes from the thoughts that we can carefully plant or remove. We can either choose to allow ourselves to be defeated by failure or we can dust ourselves off and get up, learn the lesson, move on. The real debate around failure goes on in our mind. Because we get to blame ourselves, we get to feel ashamed, we get to feel guilty, we get to feel miserable. And this can ruin your mood and eventually it can terminate your road to success. If you allow negative thinking to affect you, then you can kiss your journey to success goodbye.

Your mindset will give you the tools to cope with anything that may come your way. Your mindset can set you up for success or it can bring you off the path.

Your way of thinking will have such a great impact on you that your way to success will either be straight forward or it will throw you off.

Constantly working on your mindset and your way of thinking will make you understand more clearly what is the mechanics behind success. Your mind can keep you motivated if you strengthen your mindset in a way that will only focus your attention on solutions. But at the same time your mind can easily sabotage you if your attention tends to be focused on problems that seem to have no escape.

The truth is, our mindset can become a trap if we do not take care of it. It can be offering you tools to succeed and accomplish your goals or it can throw you in the middle of the storm and take you away the umbrella so that you are convinced that failure is inevitable. But what happens is that your thoughts can exaggerate a situation to such an extent that you might see a small setback as an inevitable failure that you will never ever be able to overcome.

How do you achieve a strong and healthy mindset?

You can work on it by yourself or you can reach out for help. There are so many inspirational and motivational books, videos, events, speakers, summits, conferences out there. The offering is wide and complex, it is your choice what suits you best and what fits your lifestyle. Sometimes we need to hear the same thing over and over again and it will only click when we hear it from a certain person. So go out there and explore the possibilities that you have to improve your mindset. And most importantly keep in mind that there will always be more space for improvement. We are complex human beings, we grow, we evolve and we need always pay attention to our inner and outer development. We are in a constant evolution and we are improving ourselves, our health, our bodies, our mind, our spirituality and so on. We learn for as long as we live.

The importance of strengthening your mindset will be decisive in the long run to whether you will succeed or not, to the way you approach opportunities, to the confidence that you will display or to the way you recover after failure. If you allow your negative thoughts to take over, you will find yourself in a position of giving up and you might regret it afterwards. It is never too late to start all over again, once you have learned the lesson, but if you work on your mindset, you will not need to give it all up and take a break before starting it all over again. You will go with it constantly, you will build on top of the failures and you will always see the bright light at the end of the tunnel. This is more than just being optimistic, this is about having the mindset of a successful person.

CHAPTER 5: YOUR STRATEGY TO SUCCESS

"A vision without a strategy remains an illusion." **Lee Bolman**

Once you have defined what success means to you and how it looks like and once you have developed your mindset to keep you in a strong process, you are ready to take the next step. As with every goal and objective you set, this is the exciting time when you need to start planning.

Creating a plan when you have a goal in mind is all about being very specific. You need to break down your goal into actionable items. Your roadmap to succeeding in your pursuit towards your goal will be set up with a very clear strategic approach. You need to be specific in each step that needs to be taken.

When planning to reach an objective, it is essential to have a deadline in mind. Sometimes you may need to be flexible, but it helps when putting your strategy in place to decide what is your timeline. You can start working backwards from the deadline you set up for your goals and see if it is achievable or what are the adjustments you need to make.

Creating a blueprint for your goal is that exciting phase when you hold your vision of success in mind and create from it. You are free at this stage to be as creative and open as possible. You can dream big, you can look at opportunities with excitement and focus your mindset on the every day wins. You are flexible to make any changes in this stage and you can create the strategy that will bring you success in your goals.

The beauty of creating roadmaps is that you have the big picture in mind. When you start the process it is easy to get lost in the details and every little task that needs to be done, but in this strategy phase, you are creating the big picture. Success is accessible and you are now the master of your roadmap to achieve it.

With a strong thinking and an open mind, there is nothing that will be stopping you. Because everything can make you see beyond the appearance, you can spot an opportunity in a place where you never even thought about. You are focused on success and everything is a possibility. How wonderful is that?

Your strategy to success needs to be YOURS. You need to remember that you do not have to follow a recipe or a formula to achieve success. You are free to experiment and do things your own way because only by trying what feels suitable, you will be able to admit what works and what does not work. Otherwise it will just be easy to blame the system or the formula that did not work and give up because you have no idea what else to do and how to adapt your strategy.

But if you are focused from the beginning on what you want to create and achieve and how you want to get there, then you will be aware of the steps you need to take, you will have ownership of all the little pieces that need to fall into place for the vision to start coming to life.

"Success is 20% skills and 80% strategy. You might know how to succeed, but more importantly, what's your plan to succeed?" Jim Rohn

When you put down the plan, your goals seem to

get closer. Your success becomes more real when you look at it from the perspective of the strategy that you have created. When you have a strategy in place, you will be ready for facing any setbacks and failures. When your strategy is clear and you know what you are after, then your success will be a beautiful outcome. The plan gets to be your guiding roadmap.

The strategy to success is like driving to a destination. When you are going on a new route and expecting to reach a completely new destination that you have never before visited, then you need a map. You need a GPS with clear coordinates that will guide you step by step, with all the turnings to left and right. This will give you peace of mind and will keep you on the road in order to not miss your destination and in order to not get distracted and stop along the way.

By creating a strategy, you are more inclined to succeed. Otherwise, what is the point of having a goal in mind but no clue how to get there? Sooner or later you will push yourself to create a plan and later on you will get the chance to refine your strategy, to learn from the mistakes and to adapt according to the results.

Planning it out will just be a helping hand to create a more realistic perspective of the success you have in mind. You know you can achieve it, you are thinking about it all the time, and now it is time to connect the dots and create the roadmap. Set your milestones. Plan the timeline. Think about the risks. Think about the solutions that you can adopt. Think about the good parts and think about the bad parts. Consider everything you need to consider because now you are in the place of planning when you can still modify without any impact. Later on, you will still be able to make adjustments, but you will need to take into consideration some additional aspects in order to incorporate all that is already involved.

Make your strategy personal, you are the creator of your roadmap, you know best what aligns with your goals and vision. Stay on top of it and be flexible. Create a strategy that allows room for improvement, given that it is an unknown and uncertain ground that you are stepping on and you need to make sure to learn and grow, to develop but eventually to reach the success.

CHAPTER 6: IMPLEMENT YOUR STRATEGY

"The path to success is to take massive, determined action." – Tony Robbins

Alright, so now you have a strategy in place. Your plan looks strong and you have considered all possible scenarios you could think of. You are prepared for any surprises and you know that you have the mindset of a winner.

Statistics show that many people who wanted to become successful created a plan, but they never had the courage to implement it. And their dreams died without even trying. Their shot at success was cut before even having an attempt of being put into practice.

Many great minds talk about success in terms of the action that is being taken. It is the effort and the steps that create the path.

"I never did anything worth doing by accident, nor did any of my inventions come indirectly through accident, except the phonograph. No,

when I have fully decided that a result is worth getting, I go about it, and make trial after trial, until it comes." -- Thomas Edison

When starting to implement your strategy, the main point is to never give up. Constantly trying and pushing through whatever comes, "trial after trial" will bring you closer to success.

"Successful people maintain a positive focus in life no matter what is going on around them. They stay focused on their past successes rather than their past failures, and on the next action steps they need to take to get them closer to the fulfillment of their goals rather than all the other distractions that life presents to them." - Jack Canfield

Action is a very important ingredient in the recipe for success. You are not really getting any closer to success if you do not take action. Implementing the plan that you put onto paper or in a presentation on your computer can either stay as a plan or it can be transformed into reality. Success is only possible by taking action.

"The key to success is action, and the essential in action is perseverance." -- Sun Yat-sen

When you make the decision to follow your plan, you need to keep going. Perseverance will make you take action all the time and push through, no matter how many times you fail. You may hit low points when you think about "what is the reason for doing all of this", but that is when your strong mindset needs to take over and create the reality. Because in these situations, the reality will be blurry and you might feel defeated. But you need to see beyond the small problem and keep implementing the actions.

The reason why the strategy creation is a very important part of your success is that you create the roadmap so that when it comes to implementing it, you have all the steps and all you need to do is follow the plan. This will give you a sense of certainty. At least up to one point when you are going to adapt your strategy if needed. Nevertheless, your strategy will be the one to dictate what actions you need to take in order to get closer to your objectives and achieve your goals. After all, it is about the goal and everything you put into action has to reflect small wins that bring you closer to a successful outcome.

Most of the times, it will be tempting to give up. Feeling tired and overwhelmed or not seeing the expected results will make you wish for an easy escape. Giving up is the easiest. Then you can just return to your comfort zone and you do not need to worry about uncertainty and overwhelm. But that means giving up your goal and your dreams of a successful life as well.

The stage of implementation is the longest one, it can be a bumpy road some of the times, but it can also be very rewarding some other times. Until you start reaching constant results and success, this is the stage that you will need to keep doing: implementing your strategy by taking constant action. After all, you cannot really know what can happen unless you really do something in that direction, right?

"Action is a great restorer and builder of

confidence. Inaction is not only the result, but the cause, of fear. Perhaps the action you take will be successful; perhaps different action or adjustments will have to follow. But any action is better than no action at all." -- Norman Vincent Peale

Taking action and implementing the steps you have envisioned will make you feel scared, will produce fear and it will make you feel inappropriate. But at the same time it will make you feel confident and powerful because you have actioned after all and that is what will differentiate you from the people who will not succeed, simply because they chose the comfort of not doing anything and you took the risk, you plunged into the fear and you acted.

The strategy boosts your confidence and trust in your potential and then you add your skills in order to start producing magic. Some of the times, you may not see the results and it will seem that all the action is in vain. But it is not. There will be situations in which results will be late to appear, but each and every action will build the momentum and it will build the foundation, brick after brick, for your win that follows.

"Success comes from taking the initiative and following up... persisting... eloquently expressing the depth of your love. What simple action could you take today to produce a new momentum toward success in your life?" -- Tony Robbins

If you hurry up and do not break down your strategy into actionable steps, you will find it confusing at the beginning. Because you will not know what to start with. You will just see all these steps that need to be taken, but you have no idea in which order. You have no clue by when you need to complete some of the actions in order to be able to meet the deadline. In this case, you will be overwhelmed before you even start. The risk runs high that you will delay in taking action for the simple fact that you will feel like you have no idea what you are doing.

Strategy and implementation go hand in hand. The purpose of creating a very good and clear strategy is to support you in the implementation phase. And when you have a solid strategy, then you can return after any implemented step and look at what needs to be done next.

Once things start moving, then you get momentum and one win after the other will help you see the light at the end of the tunnel. You will start rolling the dices and you will also gain more confidence. Therefore, you will be taking more and more actions and your mindset will improve with each win.

"Any action is often better than no action, especially if you have been stuck in an unhappy situation for a long time. If it is a mistake, at least you learn something, in which case it's no longer a mistake. If you remain stuck, you learn nothing."
-- Eckhart Tolle

All the steps that we will be implementing will offer some learning points. Sometimes we need to allow ourselves to learn as we go. Instead of feeling defeated and wanting to give up, just dig in after your mindset, your confidence and your trust and keep going. Find ways, find new solutions, find alternatives.

"You see, in life, lots of people know what to do,

but few people actually do what they know. Knowing is not enough! You must take action." -- Tony Robbins

Creating the strategy to success is the stage where you put down what you know. You know what you have to do, you know the steps that need to be taken and you know the skills that are required. Now all it takes is to do it. And that is why the implementation stage is scary and difficult. It is the stage where most people give up. What if you know what needs to be done to achieve your success and choose to sit in your corner and dream about it? Who will benefit from you dreaming about your success? Think about the people that would benefit instead from your following the path, putting into action all those ideas, acquiring the skills, learning, and doing. Constantly taking action and being proactive. There is that saying that when a door closes, you need to find a window and jump in. This is how you constantly stay in an action – taking mode and look for solutions.

If you keep your knowledge to yourself, you are choosing to be selfish. You are choosing to just keep it inside and not share it. Your fear prevents you from being successful and at the same time it prevents you from making an impact in the world.

Keep this in mind, implementing your strategy will be a long journey and it will keep changing and evolving and growing, but so will you. And this way you will get to your success because without taking action and implementing the steps required, there is no success to be enjoyed. Sooner or later, the results will start appearing and they will be in direct proportion with the amount of action that you have taken. So keep at it, it will pay off eventually. Implement, implement, implement!

CHAPTER 7: HOW TO OVERCOME OBSTACLES

As already mentioned in the previous chapter, taking action will sometimes lead to unexpected results or even failure. There will be setbacks and there will be obstacles, no matter how many risks have been evaluated in the strategic phase and no matter how many scenarios have been imagined. Reality sometimes can slap us in the face and we need to deal with it.

"Obstacles don't have to stop you. If you run into a wall, don't turn around and give up. Figure out how to climb it, go through it, or work around it." – Michael Jordan

The whole purpose of challenges that come our way is to learn how to overcome them and to allow them to teach us a lesson instead of seeing them as threatening and run away from them. Face them, look them in the eyes. Treat obstacles as an advantage and an opportunity to learn the lesson you needed to learn.

If that obstacle had not happened, then you might have gone all the way without learning something useful. Maybe you would have learned it later on, but why not do it now, when the challenge is here and you have the chance to figure out how to overcome it.

Whenever you meet an obstacle, your first instinct might be to give up. It is the simple way out after all and we are built to look for the emergency exit when things go wrong. But your healthy and strong mindset will instead help you to see the things from a new perspective. You are not like everyone else and you will not give up. Instead you will stay motivated and find the power inside of you to move on. You will find a way to get over the tough situation. Our mind likes being triggered to find creative solutions. In the first moments when hitting a challenge, your first reaction will tend to be of panic. But once you become more experienced this will not be so persistent anymore. Once you get over panic, your mind goes into rescue mode and starts looking for solutions. The problem in front of you is now like an interesting puzzle that needs to be solved. You can see it as an exciting opportunity to put your creativity to work. Sooner or later there will be some solutions coming up that might even surprise you because you would have never seen them unless you were open to creating them.

"I've always found that anything worth achieving will always have obstacles in the way and you've got to have that drive and determination to overcome those obstacles on route to whatever it is that you want to accomplish." -- Chuck Norris

The truth is that victory is sweeter when you have overcome all the obstacles in the way. It is quite impossible to have a smooth sailing towards success. It might mean that you have chosen a goal that is too small. You know what they say, if it does not scare you then you need to change your goal. And of course then the bigger the goal, the more probable it becomes that you will need to face uncertainty and blockages, but you will not remain stuck. The determination to reach success will push you to find solutions and once you get to your objective, you will truly celebrate it with a party.

The moment you hit an obstacle, you need to return to your roadmap. If it is something you have been prepared for and you have already calculated as a risk, then follow the alternative plan. If it is something completely unexpected, then switch to creative thinking and analyse what can happen. Figure it out.

"When it is obvious that the goals cannot be reached, don't adjust the goals, adjust the action steps." – Confucius

Sometimes, it might seem that instead of getting closer to your goal, you are getting further and further away from it. That is a crucial moment in your journey. Because you are tested and all your beliefs around your success are tested. You might want to diminish your vision, you might want to play it small and safe, and go for something less exciting. This is when you need to be stubborn and determined. You do not need to adjust your goals. Your objective is your dream and you need to keep at it. Stay focused. Instead, analyse the situation and start adapting the action steps. Go back into strategy mode and pencil down alternative actions.

It is important to stay focused on the goals because we might find it easier to just reduce them in order to make sure we are going to hit the target. Like in a bow and arrow contest, you bring the target closer to make sure you reduce the chances to fail. That is not the answer . Playing it small is not the answer. Why not up your game and challenge yourself? If it is more difficult, then it is worth it, it becomes more valuable. Ever since the beginning of the world, we as human beings are tempted by what we cannot have. So this means that an obstacle will only make the goal more desirable. Your success will be much more delicious because you know all the effort that went in to create all the steps and figure it all out along the way.

Keep this close whenever you need some additional motivation and inspiration for overcoming obstacles:

"Courage sometimes is the quietest voice

That roars loudest from within,

Making faith a distinctive choice

And compelling motivation to try again.

When obstacles invariably come your way,

Into every direction that you have turned,

A thousand misery comes in a friendlier display

To take away the strength that you have gained.

Faith stands strong like a colossal wall of courage,

Ready to do the things that you could not do.

Bold in confidence with a conquering message,

Making difficult boundaries appeared new.

You can go on overcoming obstacles,

Which at first looked almost impossible,

Success is not worth having if there are no mistakes,

There is an ability that lies beyond the solar pole."

Overcoming Obstacles -----Poem by Gerry Legister

Every obstacle that you will encounter will be a test for you and your courage. Because each challenge will require a dose of risk and taking a decision that you have never taken before. But you need to be comfortable with taking decisions in the blind, you need to be comfortable with taking risks and experimenting. This is the only way to find solutions that no one else has ever thought of. This is what will set you apart from the crowd.

Your courage will be the first skill you need to put in practice and the first skill to inject in your mindset when you set yourself on the journey to success. It will not be easy, but it will definitely be worth it. You will kick it off every single time with the right amount of courage. Although it might seem that the obstacles are delaying your from getting to the destination of success, you have to trust that you are on the right way and that you will get there at the right time.

Forcing things will only interfere with the process and you need to learn to see the obstacles as lessons and to enjoy them. Learning is the most valuable way to reach success and to keep growing. Because you already know that success is not about the destination, it is about the journey and it is also about continuing with it, keeping the momentum and not falling down from the high level of achievements. Persistence applies not only in taking action and implementing your strategy but also in overcoming obstacles and making sure you do not allow yourself to be defeated.

CHAPTER 8: EVALUATE

While implementing step by step the strategy and the action, you will need to take small breaks and include an evaluation stage. Analysing and looking where you are at in your roadmap, where you are in terms of milestones, timeline and all the small goals. Evaluation is a must in order to keep track of where you are at in the big scheme of things.

When creating your strategy, you need to make sure to include in your timeline the periodic stages of evaluating. This will give you a moment to breathe and drag a line and calculate what has happened and what needs to happen further on. Analysing the health of your goals is very powerful. You already know that the obstacles will be there no matter what and you will adjust your actions along the way. That is why you need to have these breathing moments to look back and revisit your strategy.

Making adjustments to the actions that you are taking might result in changes that you need to make to the bigger plan. Maybe something that you were planning to do much later down the line needed to be brought to our attention sooner. So you need to look at the roadmap and make the overall changes based on the impact that might result.

Any successful project needs to have stages of evaluation spread across the implementation of the strategy and as part of the milestones. In fact, a good idea is to establish a review after hitting each milestone. This way, you will be able to review from a place of having just won something. You will look at things and decide what needs to be improved, what works just fine and what is lacking.

When finding yourself in the moment of evaluation, you need to consider a few aspects. First of all, you look at where you are at on the roadmap in comparison to your estimated situation for this stage. When you have created your strategy, you had the milestones planned and by this point in time you were supposed to be in a certain position. So you have the estimated outcome that you can measure against the real outcome at the present moment.

Then you can start looking back at the previous steps. What actions have been taken, what steps have been implemented so far and what obstacles have been defeated along the way. Look at whether there is something right now preventing you to move forward. Analyse the actions that lead to this result at this particular milestone. Is there something you could have done better? Is there something that went just exactly as planned? Is there something that did not quite go as according to plan, but still managed to create a positive result? Is there something that went terribly wrong that made you adjust a lot of the actions that followed up? Drag a line and see what is the score. How many wins, how many losses so far.

If you are in the point where you were expecting yourself to be, then that is brilliant. Keep going. If you find yourself in a delay when it comes to your timeline to success, then you need to check closer what brought you here and if there is something that is keeping you stuck.

Become creative right now at this point. This is when you need to look at the next actions. In most cases, the initial strategy will no longer be applicable at this point, but that is ok because this is what the role of the evaluation is all about.

Revisit what was initially planned to happen as the next steps. Perhaps the actions are still good to be taken into consideration, maybe you need to slightly adjust the order of the steps. Or maybe you need to scrap off everything and figure out a completely new way moving forward because you are facing a new puzzle. Your successful milestone might have brought some additional risks that you have not considered at the beginning so now they need to be evaluated and act accordingly.

Create a new roadmap if you must. After all, it is much better to create new steps and look at the situation from an inspired perspective and considering new options rather than sticking with the original plan that clearly feels wrong. The whole journey and strategy to success is about being flexible. Remember when I mentioned that in a previous chapter? This is where flexibility comes in handy. And of course it all ties in with the mindset. Because if you are too attached to the initial plan, you might become stubborn when it comes to changing it. And that will just affect the process, because stubbornness is not healthy. Flexibility and keeping an open mind is what will be a more realistic approach and what will drive you closer to success.

At this point of evaluating, do not forget to celebrate the wins. Also, when it comes to the setbacks and reviewing what went wrong, refrain yourself from trying to find a guilty part or someone to blame the mistake on. It will not be productive, especially if the crisis has already passed. Remind yourself of the lesson, perhaps you need to remind your team of the lessons and be appreciative of their efforts that lead to pushing through and overcoming the obstacle.

Keep a positive note and focus all the time on the good side of things, no matter if they are wins or if they are failures. In the big picture, they are still considered to be an additional step in your journey that you have put together for accomplishing your goals. Your strategy is safe and needs to be reviewed periodically so remember to be flexible and always on the lookout for creative solutions that will keep the momentum going and the speed to a high level.

CHAPTER 9: SUCCESS IS ACTION

This is not new, we have already mentioned and underlined the importance of action in the process of achieving success. This time we are focusing on the continuous progress of the journey.

Sometimes it can happen that a review of the situation might bring to attention some pressure. The feeling of confusion might kick in. But the crucial part is to keep on moving. Yes, take a break and rest, restore your energy if you need to, but never take the foot off the acceleration. Even if it is small actions that you are taking, it is still better to do something every single day that will bring you closer to a better tomorrow.

"It's the action, not the fruit of the action, that's important. You have to do the right thing. It may not be in your power, may not be in your time, that there will be any fruit. But that doesn't mean you stop doing the right thing. You may never know what results come from your action. But if you do

nothing, there will be no result." -- Mahatma Gandhi

Keeping the momentum going is what will save you from falling off the grid. Small steps are better than no steps. Even if you are not sure of what you are doing, this does not mean that it will prevent you. Courage will show you the way. Just keep on doing. Because sitting and watching will not take you anywhere.

"Often we are caught in a mental trap of seeing enormously successful people and thinking they are where they are because they have some special gift. Yet a closer look shows that the greatest gift that extraordinarily successful people have over the average person is their ability to get themselves to take action." -- Anthony Robbins

In almost all cases, it is more important to just take action although it may not be the right action. Leaders need to make decisions every day. And sometimes they are not right. Sometimes they have no idea what they are doing. Sometimes they are just taking a shot in the dark. But they need to make a decision, because they are there to lead. And staying in uncertainty will not move the needle in any direction.

Be confident that no matter what action you take, it is going to sort itself out and it will bring you on the right path. This is not about being right or wrong, and it certainly is not about proving anything to anybody. In fact, it might be our own ego that prevents us to take any type of action. We are afraid of what others will think. We are afraid of what others will be judging us for. We are afraid most of all of what we are going to judge ourselves for. We allow this fear to freeze us in place and this is a dangerous place to be. Instead, just make a move. It does not have to be right or wrong. But it will keep you in movement.

After overcoming challenges and obstacles, we are tempted to sit back and relax and think that it has passed, but we need to keep on going. Evaluating our actions will give us a direction of movement, but sometimes we need to act in the spur of the moment and really make a decision. If you are based on a strong and healthy mindset, then you will own any aftermath and consequences. You will face whatever result will unfold. Because you made the decision and created movement and that is more important than anything else.

It is really essential to keep in mind that taking action will save you from the moments of thinking "what if" and having regrets. Why would you choose to evaluate something that you did not act upon when instead you can deal with the results because at least the results are real and not imaginary.

"Don't let the expectations and opinions of other people affect your decisions. It's your life, not theirs. Do what matters most to you; do what makes you feel alive and happy. Don't let the expectations and ideas of others limit who you are. If you let others tell you who you are, you are living their reality — not yours. There is more to life than pleasing people. There is much more to life than following others' prescribed path. There is so much more to life than what you experience right now. You need to decide who you are for yourself. Become a whole being. Adventure." — Roy T. Bennett

You are creating your own reality and your own story. You are allowed to make any decisions you want. You are allowed to make mistakes. You are carving your own success.

CHAPTER 10: CELEBRATE YOUR SUCCESS

You made it! You are seeing win after win. Yes, there are some small setbacks along the way, but the balance is pretty clear that it is in favour of your success.

This is a very important step of the journey. Because it is something we have already discussed, that success is not a destination, it is an ongoing journey. And it is important to stay awake during the journey and keep a positive attitude. Therefore, each win, no matter how small or big, needs to be celebrated. Do not wait for the big success to hit you because you will have created too much tension and pressure and no matter how big the party will be, you will not be able to enjoy it fully. Instead keep celebrating along the way, put a little bit of a party and a feeling of high energy into it every day.

It will actually even make a big difference when it comes to facing the failures and obstacles. Why not celebrate them too? Because if you look at them more carefully, you realise they are the most useful lessons that push you further and sometimes without these challenges we risk to not grow. Celebrate it even if it does not look like a successful result. It is still a result and what do you know, maybe it is success disguised in failure because you have been too attached to your own idea of success.

Taking time to celebrate sometimes feels like a waste because you need to stay focused. But the truth is that when you keep the pressure up, no good will come out of it. This is mainly because you will be trapped in a worrying mode and instead of focusing to search for the wins, you are too deep into the darkness. Having a perspective of celebration and feeling good with the journey will always make you look out for the wins. It will make the journey more pleasurable and it will help you be in a rewarding mode when milestones are hit and small wins come your way. Live them. Breathe them. Be passionate. Do not overlook the little victories, as they are the ones that are building the path to the highest level of success.

"Celebrate every success, but don't forget to enjoy those scars of failures." – Debasish Mridha

Has it ever occurred to you that life is too short to not celebrate? Yes, you are pursuing your goals and you are on a mission to achieve success, but life is happening during this whole time. And you need to really enjoy it.

"The most beautiful things are not associated with money; they are memories and moments. If you don't celebrate those, they can pass you by." -- Alek Wek

You certainly do not want life to pass you by while you are striving to accomplish your goals. Success is in the whole journey and needs to be celebrated constantly. You have so many things to be grateful for every day, that it would be a shame not to celebrate constantly. Life is too short to stay so busy that you forget about the little joys.

If you are surrounded by a team of people helping and supporting you in your journey to success, then you are responsible to make their lives happier too.

Because a happy team will perform better and they will support you from a place of caring and loving and appreciating you. Be generous in appraisals, keep a good and positive environment and always remember to celebrate the win of the day.

Most the times, people choose to focus on the problems and they get so stuck in that thinking mode that they miss out on the great stuff happening around them.

If you are working on achieving success in your relationships, every type of interaction is a win. Every conversation, every meaningful comment and every connection is precious and worthy of a party! Maybe this is too much, but you can define your own type of party. Just do not skip it because it will lift up your mood. And the chances are that when you are in a good mood, you get more creative, you can overcome obstacles faster and you are more successful overall. It is a continuous circle and it will always be in the advantage of everyone to celebrate.

"We all have life storms, and when we get the

rough times and we recover from them, we should celebrate that we got through it. No matter how bad it may seem, there's always something beautiful that you can find." -- Mattie Stepanek

When you have a bad day and it feels like you are constantly failing, make it your mission to find a positive side of things. Make it your mission to celebrate something good that has happened because it most probably slipped your attention while you were focus on the anger and frustration of failing. Changing the perspective from where you are looking at life will give you a major shift in your mood and it will challenge you to find the silver lining. After all, we could stay in our bed and complain all day long, we all have our own issues, but how about we leave those behind and look at the good aspects? Our energy will increase, we will feel so much better and motivated to keep taking action, to keep succeeding. After all, we are celebrating success and looking forward to generate even more success.

"It's important to celebrate your failures as much as your successes. If you celebrate your

failures really well, and if you get to the motto and say, 'Wow, I failed, I tried, I was wrong, I learned something,' then you realize you have no fear, and when your fear goes away, you can move the world." -- Sebastian Thrun

How beautiful it is to walk your journey to success by celebrating? You have a strong strategy, you have a well defined goal and you know what success means to you. Your healthy mindset keeps you motivated and inspired, you are productive, you are creative and always find solutions to overcome the obstacles. You evaluate, make adjustments, keep an open mind and stay flexible because you know that acting stubborn will only get in your own way to succeeding. You keep doing the great job and you keep taking fearless action and this way you get closer and closer to success and then you can keep thinking about increasing your goals. In all this process, celebration has to be an integrated part and it has to stay in the best shape so that your agenda makes you excited every day.

Now it is your turn. What is success to you? How are you going to create the plan and what actions can you start taking along the way? And while we are at it, how about you come up with an idea to celebrate the beginning of this journey, because this will give you a boost of energy. Celebrate and enjoy the journey to success!

Text Copyright © Steve Van Gard

All rights reserved. No part of this book may be reproduced in any form without permission in writing from the publisher except in the case of brief quotations embodied in critical articles or reviews.

www.ingramcontent.com/pod-product-compliance
Lightning Source LLC
Chambersburg PA
CBHW052339220526
45472CB00001B/501